by Tony Bove

Wiley Publishing, Inc.

iPod® & iTunes® For Dummies®, Pocket Edition
Published by
Wiley Publishing, Inc.
111 River Street
Hoboken, NJ 07030-5774
www.wiley.com

Published by Wiley Publishing, Inc., Indianapolis, Indiana
Published simultaneously in Canada

For general information on our other products and services, please contact our Customer Care Department within the U.S. at 800-762-2974, outside the U.S. at 317-572-3993, or fax 317-572-4002.

For technical support, please visit www.wiley.com/techsupport.

Wiley also publishes its books in a variety of electronic formats. Some content that appears in print may not be available in electronic books.

Pocket Edition ISBN: 978-0-470-42188-8

Manufactured in the United States of America

Contents at a Glance

Publisher's Acknowledgments

We're proud of this book; please send us your comments through our online registration form located at `www.dummies.com/register/`.

Some of the people who helped bring this book to market include the following:

Acquisitions, Editorial, and Media Development

Project Editors: Paul Levesque

Sr. Acquisitions Editor: Bob Woerner

Copy Editors: Virginia Sanders

Editorial Manager: Leah Cameron

Cartoons: Rich Tennant, `www.the5thwave.com`

Composition Services

Project Coordinator: Kristie Rees

Layout and Graphics: Stacie Brooks, Kathie Rickard

Proofreaders: Laura Bowman, Caitie Kelly

Publishing and Editorial for Technology Dummies

Richard Swadley, Vice President and Executive Group Publisher

Bob Ipsen, Vice President and Group Publisher

Joseph Wikert, Vice President and Publisher

Publishing for Consumer Dummies

Diane Graves Steele, Vice President and Publisher

Joyce Pepple, Acquisitions Director

Composition Services

Gerry Fahey, Vice President of Production Services

Debbie Stailey, Director of Composition Services

Introduction

You don't need much imagination to see why so many people are so happy with their iPods, or why hundreds of millions of iPods have been sold as of this writing. Imagine no longer needing to take CDs or DVDs with you when you travel — your favorite music and videos fit right in your pocket, and you can leave your precious content library at home.

What's more, this library is stored in electronic form (and is easily backed up to other media), so it never deteriorates — unlike CDs, DVDs, and other physical media that may last only a few decades.

When I first encountered the iPod, it came very close to fulfilling my dream as a road warrior — in particular, the dream of filling up a car with music as easily as filling it up with fuel. For example, I use a fully loaded iPod with my car using a custom in-vehicle interface adapter that offers an iPod connector; or I use a cassette adapter, or even an FM radio transmitter, in a rental car or boat. Whether you want to be *On the Road* with Jack Kerouac (in audio book form) or "Drivin' South" with Jimi Hendrix, just fill up your iPod or iPhone and go!

About This Book

I designed this *iPod & iTunes For Dummies,* Pocket Edition, as a reference so that you can easily find the information you need right when you need it. Now, if you'd prefer to read the book straight through, from beginning to end, feel free. That'd be another way to find out how to use iTunes and your iPod from scratch. And just to keep as many of your options open as possible, I also organized this book so that you can dive in anywhere and begin reading the info you need to know for each task.

I don't have enough pages to cover every detail of every function of the software, and I intentionally leave out some detail so that you're not befuddled with technospeak when it's not necessary. (Really, engineers can sometimes provide too many obscure choices that no one ever uses; on the other hand, I did need gapless playback.) I write brief but comprehensive descriptions and include lots of cool tips on how to get the best results from using your iPod.

Conventions Used in This Book

Like any book that covers computers and information technology, this book uses certain conventions:

- **Choosing from a menu:** When I write "Choose iTunes⇨Preferences in iTunes," you click iTunes on the toolbar and then choose Preferences from the iTunes menu.

  With the iPod, when you see "Choose Extras⇨Calendars from the iPod main menu," you highlight Extras in the main menu with the scroll wheel, press the Select button to select Extras, and then highlight and select Calendars from the Extras menu.

- **Clicking and dragging:** When you see "Drag the song over the name of the playlist," I mean you need to click the song name, hold the mouse button down, and then drag the song with the mouse over to the name of the playlist before lifting your finger off the mouse button.
- **Keyboard shortcuts:** When you see ⌘-I, press the ⌘ key on a Mac keyboard along with the appropriate shortcut key. (In this case, press I, which opens the Song Information window in iTunes.) In Windows, the same keyboard shortcut is Ctrl-I (which means press the Ctrl key along with the I key).
- **Step lists:** When you come across steps that you need to do in iTunes or on the iPod, the action is in **bold**, and the explanatory part follows. If you know what to do, read the action and skip the explanation. But if you need a little help along the way, check out the explanation.

And Just Who Are You?

You don't need to know anything about music or audio technology to discover how to make the most of your iPod and the iTunes software that comes with it. Although a course in music appreciation can't hurt, the iPod and iTunes are designed to be useful even for air-guitar players who barely know the difference between downloadable music and System of a Down. You don't need any specialized knowledge to have a lot of fun while building up your digital music library.

Icons Used in This Book

This book uses three icons to help you along the way:

Highlights techniques that may save you time.

Alerts you to important things you'll want to remember.

Points you to information on the companion Web site at `www.dummies.com/go/ipod6e`.

Where to Go from Here

You've got your copy of *iPod & iTunes For Dummies,* Pocket Edition — now what? This minibook is a reference, so if you need information on which version of the iPod to choose, go to Part I. If you are interested in finding out how to set up iTunes on your iPod, go to Part II. Alternatively, you can start with Part I and just read through the pages in order. If you want more advice on the iPod and iTunes, such as using advanced techniques, check out the full-sized version of *iPod & iTunes For Dummies,* 6th Edition — simply head to your local bookseller or go to `www.dummies.com`.

Part I

Firing Up Your iPod

In This Part

- Introducing the iPod
- What you need to get started
- Scrolling through the iPod main menu
- Pressing the iPod buttons

As an iPod owner, you're on the cutting edge of entertainment technology. This chapter introduces the iPod and tells you what to expect when you open the box. I describe how to power up your iPod and connect it to your computer, both of which are essential tasks that you need to know how to do — your iPod needs power, and it needs audio and video, which it gets from your computer.

Introducing the iPod

An iPod is, essentially, a hard drive or flash memory drive as well as a digital music and video player in one device. An iPod is such a thing of beauty and style — and so highly recognizable by now — that all Apple needs to do in an advertisement is show one all by itself.

The convenience of carrying music on an iPod is phenomenal. For example, the 160GB iPod classic can hold around 40,000 songs. That's more than two months of nonstop music played around the clock — or about two new songs per day for the next 54 years. And with built-in skip protection in every model, you won't miss a beat as you jog through the park or when your car hits a pothole.

A common misconception is that your iPod becomes your music and video library. Actually, your iPod is simply another *player* for your content library, which is safely stored on your computer. One considerable benefit of using your computer to organize your content is that you can make perfect-quality copies of music, videos, movies, podcasts, and audio books. You can then copy as much of the content as you want, in a more compressed format, onto your iPod and take it on the road. Meanwhile, your perfect copies are stored safely on your computer. Your favorite albums, audio books, TV shows, movies, and podcast episodes can be copied over and over forever, just like the rest of your information, and they never lose their quality. If you save your content in digital format, you'll never see your songs or videos degrade, and you'll never have to buy the content again.

The iPod experience includes *iTunes* (for Mac or Windows), which lets you synchronize content with your iPod and other devices, such as the Apple TV player for your home TV and stereo. You also use iTunes to organize your content, make copies, burn CDs, and play disc jockey without discs. I introduce iTunes in Part II.

An iPod is also a *data player,* perhaps the first of its kind. As an external hard drive, the iPod serves as a portable backup device for important data files. You can transfer your calendar and address book to help manage your affairs on the road, and you can even use calendar event alarms to supplement your iPod's alarm and sleep timer. You can keep your calendar and address book in your iPod automatically synchronized to your computer, where you normally add and edit information.

In the case of the iPod touch and iPhone, your data player is in fact a complete *personal digital assistant* that lets you enter data as well as play it. With an iPod touch or iPhone you can check and send e-mail, visit your favorite Web sites, get maps, obtain driving directions, check the current weather, and even check your stock portfolio, to name just a few things.

Comparing iPod Models

Introduced way back in the Stone Age of digital music (2001), the iPod family has grown by six generations as of this writing, with custom versions for the band U2 and offshoots such as the popular iPod nano as well as the tiny iPod shuffle that lets you wear up to 500 songs on your sleeve. Even from the beginning, iPod models were truly innovative for their times. With the MP3 music players of 2001, you could carry about 20 typical songs (or a single live Phish set) with you, but the first iPods could hold more than 1,000 typical songs (or a 50-hour Phish concert).

Today's iPod models work with iTunes on either Windows computers or Macs, but that wasn't always the case. The first-generation iPods worked only with Macs. In 2002, Apple introduced the second generation — one version for Windows and another for the Mac, using the same design for both. For the third generation (2003), Apple changed the design once again.

Third-, fourth-, fifth-, and sixth-generation iPods — as well as offshoots, such as iPod mini, iPod nano, and iPod shuffle — work with either Windows or Mac and come in a variety of hard drive or flash memory sizes. By design, you can hold an iPod in your hand while you thumb the *scroll wheel* (my generic term for scroll wheel, scroll pad, touch wheel, or click wheel). The LCD screen on full-size models offers backlighting so that you can see it in the dark. The iPhone and iPod touch let you tap the sensitive display with your finger to select items and functions, and flick with your finger to scroll or move the display.

Things You Have and Things You Need

The sixth-generation (late 2008) iPod classic box includes earphones and a USB dock adapter cable that can connect either the iPod or a dock to a computer or power adapter. You can get accessories, including Apple's Universal Dock and an AC power adapter, separately. For example, the iPod AV Connection Kit offers the adapter, AV cables, Apple Remote, and the Universal Dock with adapters for all models.

The accessories don't stop there. Docks of various sizes, shapes, and functions are available from vendors, such as Belkin, Monster, and Griffin. Some docks are combined with home speaker systems. You might also want a carrying case and some other goodies, many of which are described in this book. They're available at the online Apple Store (`www.apple.com/store`) or the physical Apple Store or other consumer electronics stores.

You also need a few things that don't come with the iPod:

- **A PC or Mac to run iTunes:** On a PC, iTunes version 8.0 requires Windows XP (with Service Pack 2 to support Apple TV and the iPhone), or either 32-bit or 64-bit editions of Windows Vista, running on a 500 MHz Pentium-class processor or faster, and a minimum of 256MB. If you intend to watch video, you need at least a 2.0 GHz Pentium-class processor or faster, and at least 512MB of RAM and 32MB of video RAM.

  With a Mac, iTunes version 8.0 will run on the newest version of Mac OS X (Leopard) as well as versions as old as 10.3.9 (Panther), but requires Mac OS X 10.4.9 (Tiger) or newer to play video; a 500 MHz G3 processor or better; and at least 256MB of RAM. If you intend to watch video, you need a 1GHz G4 processor or better, and 16MB of video RAM.

- **USB connection:** PCs must have USB 2.0 (also called a *high-powered USB*) for iPod classic, iPod nano, iPod shuffle, and fifth-generation iPods. However, you can use FireWire (IEEE 1394) with older iPod models. All current-model Macs provide USB 2.0, and all Macs provide FireWire.

For details about using USB or FireWire cables, visit this book's companion Web site at `www.dummies.com/go/ipod6e`.

- **Internet connection:** Apple recommends a broadband Internet connection to buy content and stream previews from the iTunes Store, although it is possible with a dial-up connection. At a minimum, you need some kind of Internet connection to download iTunes itself.
- **CD-R or DVD-R drive:** Without a disc burner, you can't burn your own discs. On a PC, you need a CD-R or DVD-R drive. On a Mac, you need a Combo or Super Drive to burn your own discs.
- **iTunes:** Download iTunes (version 8.0 as of this writing) for Windows or the Mac from the Apple site (`www.apple.com/itunes/download/`); it's free. See Part II for instructions.

  Older models, still available in stores and online, might include versions of iTunes as old as version 4.5 — which is fine because version 4.5 works. It just doesn't have all the features of 8.0. You can download a newer version at any time to replace it.
- **QuickTime:** QuickTime (required for video) comes with iTunes. The iTunes installer for the PC installs the newest version of QuickTime for Windows (version 7.5 as of this writing), replacing any older version you might have. Macs have QuickTime preinstalled (version 7.5 as of this writing), and Mac OS X automatically updates QuickTime if you use the Software Update feature of System Preferences in the Apple menu.

Thumbing Through the Menus

After you bring content into iTunes and update your iPod, you're ready to play. The design of the iPod classic and iPod nano lets you hold the iPod in one hand and perform simple operations by thumb. Even if you're all thumbs when pressing small buttons on tiny devices, you can still thumb your way to iPod heaven.

The iPod touch, like the iPhone, offers a multi-touch interface that lets you tap your way into iPod heaven even faster. With an iPod touch, your fingers do the walking. You can make gestures, such as flicking a finger to scroll a list quickly, sliding your finger to scroll slowly or drag a slider (such as the volume slider), pinching with two fingers to zoom out of a Web page in Safari, or pulling apart with two fingers (also known as *un-pinching*) to zoom in to the page to see it more clearly.

Your iPod touch displays the message "slide to unlock" — slide your finger across this message to unlock it. The main menu appears with the following selections:

- **Safari:** Use the Safari Web browser.
- **Calendar:** View your calendar.
- **Mail:** Check and send e-mail.
- **Contacts:** View your contacts.
- **YouTube:** List and select videos from YouTube.
- **Stocks:** Check the prices for financial stocks, bonds, and funds.
- **Maps:** View maps and get driving directions.
- **Weather:** View the weather in multiple cities.

- **Clock:** View multiple clocks and use the alarm clock, timer, and stopwatch.
- **Calculator:** A simple calculator for adding, subtracting, multiplying, dividing, and so on.
- **Notes:** Add text notes.
- **Settings:** Adjust settings for Wi-Fi, sounds, brightness, and Safari usage, as well as other settings for the device.
- **App Store:** Go to Apple's online App Store to download other Apple and third-party applications for your iPod touch or iPhone.
- **Music:** Select music playlists, artists, songs, albums, and more (including podcasts, genres, composers, audio books, and compilations). The Music button also offers Cover Flow browsing.
- **Videos:** Select videos by type (movies, music videos, TV shows, or video podcasts).
- **Photos:** Select photos by photo album or select individual photos in the Photo Library.
- **iTunes:** Go to the iTunes online store to purchase content.

After touching a button on the iPod touch display, a new page appears with more selections you can touch. In fact, you can touch every menu or button you see on the display. The iPod touch runs applications (Safari, Contacts, Calendar, YouTube, and so on), and the multitouch interface changes for each application.

For example, touch the Music button on an iPod touch to view a list of artists. After touching Music, buttons appear along the bottom of the display that you can touch to view a list of playlists, artists, songs, albums, and more. With a flick of your finger, you can scroll the list and touch selections to view the albums of an artist or the contents of an album or playlist. Touch any song to start playing it, and control buttons appear to control playback: Previous/Rewind, Play/Pause, Next/Fast-Forward, and a volume slider. Press the physical button on the front of the iPod touch to return you to the Home menu.

On the iPod classic and iPod nano models, the click wheel makes scrolling through an entire music collection quick and easy. With your finger or thumb, scroll clockwise on the wheel to scroll down a list, or counterclockwise to scroll up. As you scroll, options on the menu are highlighted. Use the Select button at the center of the wheel to select whatever is highlighted in the menu display.

Fifth-generation iPods, sixth-generation iPod classic models, the iPod nano, the iPod mini, and fourth-generation iPods (including color-display models) provide pressure-sensitive buttons underneath the top, bottom, left, and right areas of the circular pad of the wheel. These areas tilt as you press them, activating the buttons.

The iPod main menu for sixth-generation iPod classic models and the iPod nano offers the following selections:

- **Music:** Select music playlists, artists, albums, songs, genres, or composers; or select an audio book. You can also select Cover Flow to browse by cover art, as shown in Figure 1-1, or Search to search for a song or album title or artist.

- **Videos:** Select videos by video playlist or by type (movies, music videos, or TV shows).
- **Photos:** Select photos by photo album or select all photos in the photo library.
- **Podcasts:** Select podcasts by title and then select podcast episodes.
- **Extras:** View the clock, set clocks for time zones, set alarms and the sleep timer, use the stopwatch, view contacts, view your calendar, view notes, and play games.
- **Settings:** Adjust menu settings, the backlight timer, the clicker, the iPod's EQ, the date and time, and so on.
- **Shuffle Songs:** Play songs from your music library in random order.
- **Now Playing:** This selection appears only when a song is playing — it takes you to the Now Playing display.

The iPod main menu for fifth-generation models is the same, except that podcasts are found in the Music menu. The main menu for fourth-generation models is the same as for fifth-generation models, but without the Videos selection.

Figure 1-1: The Music menu on an iPod nano.

Pressing the iPod Buttons

The iPod touch responds to gestures you make with your fingers. For example, you make the following gestures to perform the following functions:

- **Drag with finger:** Scroll up or down lists slowly.
- **Flick:** Quickly scroll up or down lists.
- **Tap and hold**: While scrolling, tap and hold to stop the moving list.
- **Single tap:** Select an item to play, such as a song.
- **Double tap:** Zoom in or out with Safari and all other applications.
- **Pinch:** Zoom out of photos and Safari Web pages.
- **Unpinch:** Zoom into photos and Safari Web pages.

The buttons that appear after selecting content to play on the iPod touch perform various tasks for playing content items:

- **Previous/Rewind:** Tap once to start an item over. Tap twice to skip to the previous item (such as the previous song in an album). Touch and hold to rewind.
- **Play/Pause:** Tap to play the selected item. Tap Play/Pause when an item is playing to pause the playback.
- **Next/Fast-Forward:** Tap once to skip to the next item (such as the next song in an album). Touch and hold Next/Fast-Forward to fast-forward play.
- **Left-arrow button:** Tap to go back to the previous menu.

- **Bullet-list button (playing music):** Tap to view the contents of the album containing the song.
- **Menu button on front:** Press once to go back to the main menu.

The buttons on the click wheel on iPod classic and nano models do various tasks for song, podcast, audio book, and video playback:

- **Previous/Rewind:** Press once to start an item over. Press twice to skip to the previous item. Press and hold to rewind.
- **Menu:** Press once to go back to the previous menu. Each time you press, you go back to a previous menu until you reach the main menu.
- **Play/Pause:** Press to play the selected item. Press Play/Pause when the item is playing to pause the playback.
- **Next/Fast-Forward:** Press once to skip to the next item. Press and hold Next/Fast-Forward to fast-forward.

The buttons and click wheel can do more complex functions when used in combination:

- **Turn on the iPod.** Press any button.
- **Turn off the iPod.** Press and hold the Play/Pause button.
- **Disable the iPod buttons.** To keep from accidentally pressing the buttons, push the Hold switch to the other side so that an orange bar appears (the locked position). To reactivate the iPod buttons, push the Hold switch back to the other side so that the orange bar disappears (the normal position).

- **Reset the iPod.** You can reset the iPod if it gets hung up for some reason. (For example, it might get confused if you press the buttons too quickly.) This operation resets the iPod's operating system. It doesn't change the music or data on the iPod. To reset your iPod, see this book's appendix or the Apple support article "How to reset iPod" (`http://docs.info.apple.com/article.html?artnum=61705`).
- **Change the volume.** While playing a song (the display reads `Now Playing`), adjust the volume with the scroll wheel. Clockwise turns the volume up; counterclockwise turns the volume down. A volume slider appears on the iPod display, indicating the volume level as you scroll.
- **Skip to any point in a song, video, audio book, or podcast.** While playing an item (the display reads `Now Playing`), press and hold the Select button until the progress bar appears to indicate where you are, and then use the scroll wheel to scroll to any point in the song. Scroll clockwise to move forward and counterclockwise to move backward.

Part II
Setting Up iTunes and Your iPod

In This Part

- Installing iTunes on a Windows PC and a Mac
- Examining what you can do with iTunes
- Visiting the iTunes Store
- Setting up a store account

This part explains how to set up your iPod with iTunes on a Mac or for Windows. iTunes includes the iPod software, which provides the intelligence inside the device. iTunes is no slouch in the intelligence department either, because it immediately recognizes the type of iPod you have and installs the correct software.

Installing iTunes

If you're a Mac user, you should already have iTunes installed because all Macs sold since 2003 (and many before that time) are preinstalled with iTunes and Mac

OS X, and you also get iTunes if you install Mac OS X on an older machine. The most up-to-date version of iTunes as of this writing is version 8.0.

The version of iTunes that's provided with the Mac might be the newest version; then again, it might not be. Software updates occur very rapidly. If iTunes displays a dialog with the message that a new version of iTunes is available and asks whether you would like to download it now, click Yes to download the new version. Mac OS X not only downloads iTunes but installs it automatically.

You can set your Mac to automatically download the latest version of iTunes when it becomes available. Choose Preferences from the iTunes menu, click the General tab, and select the Check for Updates Automatically check box at the bottom of the General preferences to turn it on.

If your tastes run to Windows PCs, then you'll want to download the Windows version of iTunes from the Apple Web site (`www.apple.com/itunes/download`). Just select the appropriate version (Windows here) and then click the Download iTunes Free button, as shown in Figure 2-1. Follow the instructions to download the installer to your hard drive and then have the installer walk you through getting iTunes set up on your machine.

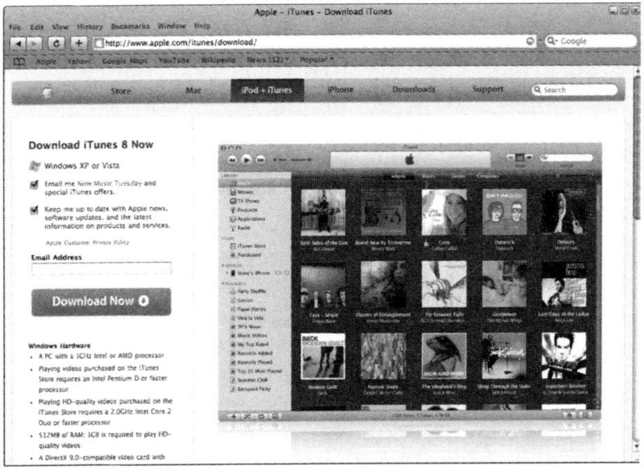

Figure 2-1: Download the newest version of iTunes from the Internet.

What You Can Do with iTunes

You can purchase songs or entire albums, audio books, TV shows, movies, and other videos from the iTunes Store and download them directly into your iTunes library, or you can copy these items from other sources (including audio CDs) into your iTunes library. You can also subscribe to *podcasts* that transfer audio or audio/video episodes, such as weekly broadcasts, automatically to your iTunes library from the Internet or through the iTunes Store. You can even use iTunes to listen to Web radio stations and add your favorite stations to your music library. After you store the content in your iTunes library, you can play it on your computer and transfer it to iPod, Apple TV, and iPhone models. You can also burn the audio content onto an audio CD or copy audio and video files onto other hard drives or DVD data discs as backups.

Transferring songs from a CD to your computer is called *ripping* a CD (to the chagrin of the music industry old-timers who think that users intend to destroy the discs or steal the songs). Ripping an entire CD's worth of songs is quick and easy, and track information, such as artist name and title, arrives automatically over the Internet for most commercial CDs. (You can add the information yourself for rare CDs, custom-mix CDs, live CDs, and others that are unknown to the database.)

You can also add video files to your iTunes library in a couple of ways: by choosing content from the iTunes Store (such as TV shows, feature-length movies, music videos, and even free movie trailers) or by downloading standard video files in the MPEG-4 format from other sources on the Internet. You can also create your own videos with a digital camcorder (or cameras built into computers, such as the iSight camera included with MacBooks) and copy them to iTunes.

As if that weren't enough, iTunes gives you the power to organize content into playlists. (You can even set up dynamic, smart playlists that reflect your preferences and listening habits.) It even has a built-in equalizer with preset settings for all kinds of music and listening environments, with the added bonus of being able to customize and save your own personalized settings with each item of content.

The Mac and Windows versions of iTunes are virtually identical, with the exception that dialogs and icons look a bit different between the two operating systems. There are also a few other differences, mostly related to the different operating environments. The Windows version lets you import Windows Media (WMA) songs; the Mac version, like most Mac applications, can be controlled by AppleScript programs. Nevertheless, as Apple continues to improve iTunes, the company releases upgrades to both versions at the same time, and the versions are free to download.

Opening the iTunes Window

You can run iTunes anytime (with or without an iPod) to build and manage your library. You don't have to actually connect your iPod until you're ready to transfer content to it.

When you launch iTunes, your library and other sources of content appear. Figure 2-2 shows the iTunes window on a PC running Windows XP, using the View as Grid pane to browse by album.

The Mac and Windows versions of iTunes look nearly identical and offer the same functions and viewing options, including the *cover browser* (also known by its older name, Cover Flow). Figure 2-3 shows the iTunes window on the Mac with the cover browser open, displaying the cover art for albums.

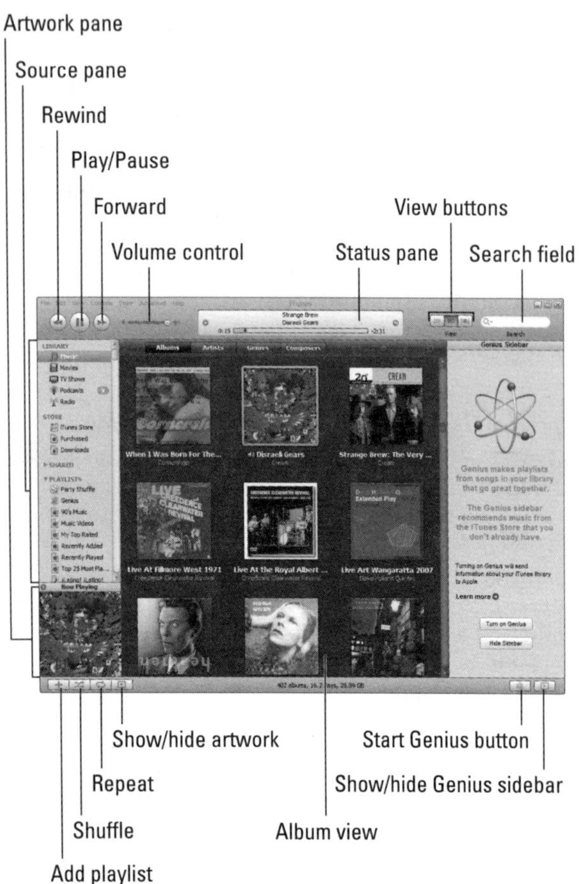

Figure 2-2: The iTunes window on a PC in Browse view.

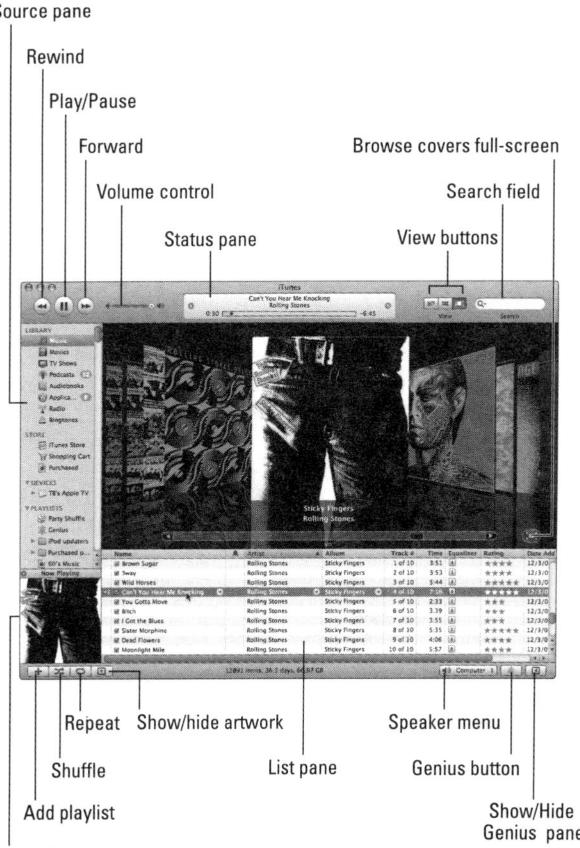

Figure 2-3: The iTunes window on a Mac with the cover browser open.

iTunes offers a view of your library and other sources for content, as well as controls for organizing, importing, and playing content, as follows:

- **Source pane:** Displays the source of content, divided into sections called Library (your music, movies, TV shows, podcasts, audio books; Store (the iTunes Store and your Purchased list); Devices (such "TB's Apple TV" in Figure 2-3); and Playlists (including Party Shuffle and your playlists).
- **Cover browser:** Also called Cover Flow, the cover browser lets you flip through your cover art to choose songs. You can use the slider (refer to Figure 2-3) to move swiftly through your library, or you can click to the right or left of the cover in the foreground to move forward or backward in your library.
- **View as List/View as Grid panes:** Depending on the source that's selected in the Source pane under Library, Store, Devices, or Playlists, these panes offer different views of the content in your library, a list of Web radio stations, the content available in the iTunes Store, the tracks of a music CD or the entire library on your iPod, or the Party Shuffle list or any one of your playlists. (Refer to Figure 2-2 for a peek at the View as Grid pane.)
- **Genius sidebar:** The Genius sidebar (refer to Figure 2-2) makes suggestions for what to get from the iTunes Store based on what you've selected. There's no obligation to buy anything, and you can open or close the Genius sidebar by clicking the boxed-arrow Show/Hide Genius Sidebar button in the lower right corner of the iTunes window.

- **View buttons:** The three buttons in the upper-right corner change your view of the List and Browse panes to show items in a list, show cover art thumbnail images in a grid, or show the cover browser.
- **Start Genius button:** The Start Genius button at the lower-right corner of the iTunes window — just to the left of the Show/Hide Genius Sidebar button — generates a playlist of songs from your library that go great with the song you selected. The Start Genius button appears only when selecting music or a playlist.
- **Status pane:** When a song, audio book, radio station, podcast, or video is playing, you see the artist name, piece title (if known), and the elapsed time displayed in this pane.
- **Search field:** Type in this field to search your library, peruse a playlist, or look in the iTunes Store.
- **Player buttons — Forward/Next, Play/Pause, and Previous/Rewind:** Use these buttons to control the playback of content in iTunes.
- **Playlist buttons — Add, Shuffle, Repeat:** Use these buttons to add playlists and shuffle or repeat playback of playlists.
- **Volume control:** You can change the volume level in iTunes by dragging the volume control slider in the upper-left section of the iTunes window to the right to increase the volume, or to the left to decrease it. The maximum volume of the iTunes volume slider is the maximum set for the computer's sound.

- **Show/Hide Artwork:** Display or hide artwork (either your own or artwork supplied with purchased songs and videos.
- **Eject button:** This button appears next to the name of an audio CD or iPod in the Source pane. To eject the CD or iPod, just click the button. Whereas a CD actually pops out of when its ejected, iPods are hard drives. So ejecting an iPod simply removes *(un-mounts)* the drive from the system.

Visiting the iTunes Store

You can visit the iTunes Store by connecting to the Internet and using iTunes. You can also click an iTunes Store link on Apple's Web site, or a similar link on any other Web site that is an iTunes affiliate with songs for sale (such as `www.rockument.com`). The link automatically launches your installed copy of iTunes and opens the iTunes Store.

As of this writing, the iTunes Store offers millions of songs, with most songs available for download for 99 cents each and entire albums available for download at less than the CD price. You can play these copy-protected songs on up to five different computers; burn CDs; and use the songs on an iPod. Apple also offers "iTunes Plus" songs and albums from some record labels (such as EMI) with higher sound quality and *without* copy protection. You can play iTunes Plus songs on just about any music player and on an unlimited number of computers — and, of course, you can burn CDs with them.

You can also buy audio books and episodes and entire seasons of TV shows. First-run movies are also available for rent or purchase. iTunes also offers tons of free content in the form of *podcasts,* which are similar to syndicated radio and TV shows, but you can download them into iTunes and play them at your convenience on your computer and on your iPod.

The iTunes Store is part of iTunes version 4 and newer, but you should be using version 7.7 as of this writing. If you're running an older version of iTunes, download the newest version, as described earlier in this part.

With the iTunes Store, you can preview any song for up to 30 seconds. Some movies offer one-minute previews and movie trailers you can view for free, and TV shows and audio books can offer previews up to 90 seconds.

If you have an account set up, you can buy and download content immediately, including movies for rent. I don't know of a faster way to purchase or rent content.

If you already have your iTunes program open, you have at least three choices when it comes to opening the iTunes Store:

- **Click the iTunes Store option in the Source pane.** The iTunes Store's home page opens, as shown in Figure 2-4.
- **Click any link in the MiniStore pane.** The iTunes Store home page opens and automatically switches your Source pane selection to iTunes Store.

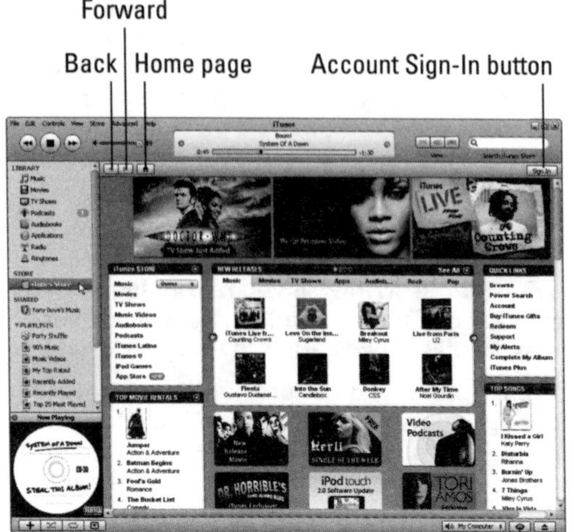

Figure 2-4: The iTunes Store home page.

- **Follow a content link in iTunes.** Click the *content link* (the gray-circled arrow next to a song or video title, artist name, or album title) to go to an iTunes Store page related to the song or video, artist, or album. iTunes searches the iTunes Store based on the item you selected. If nothing closely related turns up, at least you end up in the iTunes Store, and you might even find music you like that you didn't know about.

The iTunes Store uses the iTunes List and Browse panes to display its wares. You can check out content to your heart's content, although you can't buy content or rent movies unless you have an iTunes Store account set up. You can use the Choose Genre pop-up menu to specify music genres, or you can click links for new releases, exclusive tracks, and so on.

The iTunes Store also provides buttons on a gray bar just above the advertised content in the List pane. The left and right triangle buttons work just like the Back and Forward buttons of a Web browser, moving back a page or forward a page, respectively. The button with the Home icon takes you to the iTunes Store home page. The Browse button in the lower-right corner (refer to Figure 2-4) switches the view between Browse view (with the List and Browse panes both open) and List view (with only the List pane open).

Setting Up an Account

You need an account to purchase content or to rent movies. To create an iTunes Store account, follow these steps:

1. **In iTunes, click the iTunes Store option in the Source pane or click a music link or MiniStore pane link.**

   The iTunes Store home page appears (refer to Figure 2-4), replacing the List and Browse panes.

2. **Click the Sign In button in the upper-right corner to create an account (or sign in to an existing account).**

   When you're logged in to an iTunes account, the account name appears in place of the Sign In button. After you click the Sign In button, iTunes displays the Account Sign-In dialog.

3. **Click the Create New Account button.**

   iTunes displays a new page, replacing the iTunes Store home page with the terms of use and an explanation of the steps for creating a new account.

4. **Click the Agree button to agree with the legal terms and then click Continue.**

   iTunes displays the next page of the setup procedure, as shown in Figure 2-5.

5. **Fill in your personal account information.**

   You need to enter your e-mail address, password, test question and answer (in case you forget your password), birth date, and privacy options.

6. **Click the Continue button to go to the next page, and then enter your credit card information.**

   The entire procedure is secure, so you don't have to worry. The iTunes Store keeps your personal information (including your credit card information) on file, and you won't have to type it again.

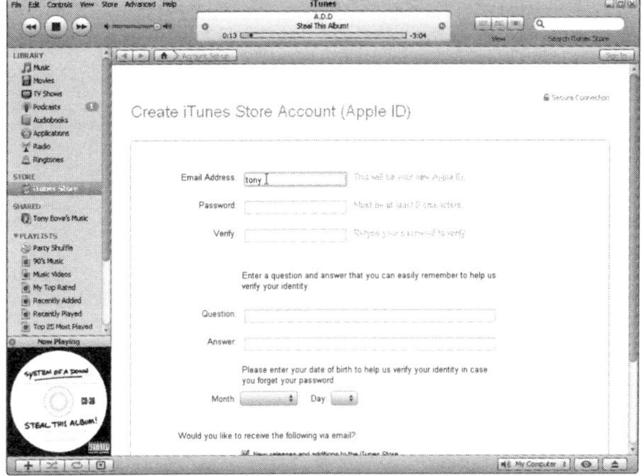

Figure 2-5: Create a new account for the iTunes Store.

7. **Click Continue to finish the procedure.**

   You can now use the iTunes Store to purchase and download content to play in iTunes and use on an iPod, iPhone, or Apple TV.

Part III
Getting Songs into Your iPod

In This Part

- Browsing and previewing songs
- Buying and downloading songs
- Setting the importing preferences
- Ripping music from CDs

With iTunes, you can put content on your iPod quickly and keep it synchronized every time you connect it. However, to put content on your iPod, you must first get it into your iTunes library.

Copyright law prohibits you from copying copyrighted content and selling it to someone else. With iTunes, however, you are allowed to make copies of music, movies, videos, audio books, and podcasts you own for your personal use, such as making backup copies on discs or hard drives, and using the content with as many iPods as you wish. However, you can't copy content from your iPod to your computer via iTunes. It's a one-way trip from iTunes to your iPod.

If you're like that guy in the movie *Diner* who couldn't stand to have his records misfiled, you'll love iTunes and its nice, neat file storage methods. For all content items, iTunes creates a folder named for the artist and then creates folders within the artist folder named for each album. These folders are stored in the iTunes Music folder unless you change your storage preferences. Content items purchased and downloaded from the iTunes Store are saved in this folder, as well as media files you drag to the iTunes window — which are copied into the iTunes Music folder without deleting the original files.

When you have the content in your iTunes library, it's a snap to automatically synchronize your iPod to your library, and away you go.

Browsing and Previewing Songs

The iTunes Store home page is loaded with specials and advertisements to peruse. To look at music in more depth, choose Music from the iTunes Store panel at the top left of the home page (next to the New Releases panel). iTunes displays more panels of advertisements and specials for music lovers. You can then choose a genre from the Genres pop-up menu on the iTunes Store panel to see only those specials and ads for a particular genre.

What if you're looking for particular music in a particular genre? You can browse the iTunes Store by genre and artist name in a method similar to browsing your iTunes library.

To browse the iTunes Store, click the Browse link in the Quick Links section of the iTunes Store home page. iTunes displays the store's offerings categorized by type of content (Such as Music), genre, and subgenre — and within each subgenre, by artist and album. Select a genre in the Genre column, then a subgenre in the Subgenre column, then an artist in the Artist column, and finally an album in the Album column, which takes you to the list of songs from that album that are available to preview or purchase, as shown in Figure 3-1.

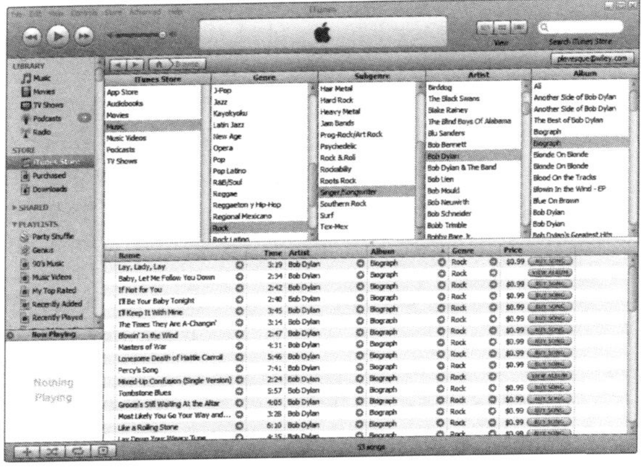

Figure 3-1: Browsing the iTunes Store for music by genre, artist, and album.

To see more information about a song or the album that it came from, click the *content link* (one of the gray-circled arrow buttons in the List pane):

- Clicking the arrow in the Artist column takes you to the artist's page of albums.
- Clicking the arrow in the Album column takes you to the album page.
- Clicking the arrow in the Name column takes you to album page with the song highlighted.

My only complaint about browsing by artist is that artists are listed alphabetically by first name. For example, you have to look up Bob Dylan under *Bob* and not *Dylan*.

To preview a song, click the song title in the List pane and then click the Play button (or press the spacebar).

By default, the previews play on your computer off the Internet in a stream, so you might hear a few hiccups in the playback. Each preview lasts about 30 seconds. Just when you start really getting into the song, it ends. If the song is irresistible, though, you can buy it on the spot.

If you know specifically what you're looking for, you can search instead of browse. The Search field in the top-right corner of the iTunes window lets you search the iTunes Store for just about anything. Type part of a song title or artist name to quickly search the iTunes Store, or use the Power Search feature to narrow your search.

Buying and Downloading Content

With Apple's 1-Click option (set by default), you click once to buy and download digital content immediately.

Alternatively, you can gather your selections in a virtual shopping cart first to see your choices and decide whether to purchase them before downloading them all at once. When you're ready to buy, you can purchase and download the items in your cart in one fell swoop.

To change your shopping method, choose iTunes⇨Preferences on a Mac or Edit⇨Preferences in Windows. In the Preferences window, click the Store button. The Store Preferences window appears. Select the Buy Using a Shopping Cart option, which turns off the 1-Click option. You can revert back to 1-Click by turning off the Buy Using a Shopping Cart option.

If you switch to the shopping cart method, the Buy button changes to an Add button — as in Add Song, Add Album, Add Episode, and so on. After adding items, you can view the selections in your shopping cart by selecting the Shopping Cart option under the iTunes Store option in the Store section of the Source pane (see Figure 3-2).

When you're ready to purchase everything in your shopping cart, click the BUY NOW button in the lower-right corner of the Shopping Cart view to close the sale and download all the items at once. Alternatively, you can click the Buy (for an album) or Buy Song button for each item that you want to purchase.

To delete items from your shopping cart, select them and press Delete/Backspace. A warning appears asking whether you're sure that you want to remove the selected items. Click Yes to go ahead and remove the selections from your shopping cart.

Figure 3-2: View your shopping cart before purchasing items from the iTunes Store.

You can see the list of all the items that you purchased by selecting the Purchased playlist under the iTunes Store option in the Source pane. The List view and Browse view change to show the items you purchased.

Adding Music from CDs

Bringing music tracks from a CD into iTunes is known as ripping a CD. I'm not sure why it's called that, but

Apple certainly took the term to a new level with an ad campaign for Macs that featured the slogan *Rip, Mix, Burn.* Burning a mix CD was the hip thing to do a few years ago. With iTunes, you can still rip and mix, but if you have an iPod, you may no longer need to burn CDs to play your music wherever you go.

Ripping, in technical terms, is extracting the song's digital information from an audio CD. In common terms, ripping also includes compressing the song's digital information and encoding it in a particular sound file format. The ripping process is straightforward, but the import settings that you choose affect sound quality, hard drive (and iPod) space, and compatibility with other types of players and computers.

Setting the importing preferences

Although importing music from an audio CD takes a lot less time than playing the CD, it still takes time. So you want your import settings to be correct before starting. Follow these steps:

Although importing music from an audio CD takes a lot less time than playing the CD, it still takes time. To minimize that time, be sure your import settings are correct before starting. To do this, follow these steps:

1. **Choose iTunes⇨Preferences⇨Advanced on a Mac or Edit⇨Preferences⇨Advanced in Windows.**

   The iTunes Preferences dialog, with the Advanced tab showing, opens.

2. **Click the Importing tab.**

   The Importing preferences appear, as shown in Figure 3-3.

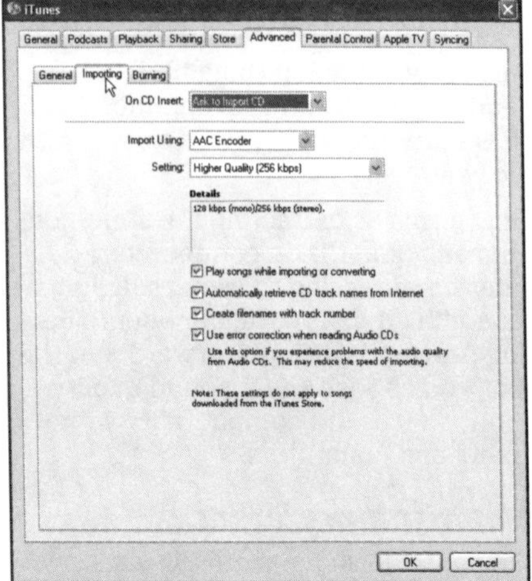

Figure 3-3: Set your importing preferences for ripping CDs.

The Importing preferences tab offers the following options, which you set before ripping a CD:

- **On CD Insert:** From this menu, choose what action iTunes should take immediately after you insert the CD. The choices are to show, play, import, or import and eject the CD.
- **Import Using:** Set this pop-up menu to one of the available encoders. This choice is perhaps the most important, and I describe it in more detail later in this section.

- **Setting:** This offers different import settings depending on your choice of encoder. You can change this setting to get better quality or use hard drive space more efficiently.
- **Play Songs While Importing or Converting:** Select this check box to play the songs at the same time you start ripping them. This option slows down the speed of importing, but hey, you get to listen to the music right away.
- **Automatically Retrieve CD Track Names from Internet:** iTunes automatically grabs the song titles, artist names, album titles, and so forth directly from an Internet database of songs. I recommend that you select this check box (assuming that you're connected to the Internet, that is).
- **Create Filenames with Track Number:** Select this check box to include the track number in the filenames created by iTunes for the songs you rip. Including the track number makes it easier to find tracks on an iPod when using a car's audio controls if you've connected your iPod to a car stereo system.
- **Use Error Correction When Reading Audio CDs:** Although you'll reduce importing speed, select this check box to use error correction if you have problems with audio quality or if the CD skips. (Not every skipping CD can be imported even with error correction, but it might help.)

For a quick and pain-free ripping session, select from among the following encoders in the Import Using pop-up menu based on how you plan to use your iTunes library:

- **AAC Encoder:** I recommend AAC for almost all music. (However, AIFF or WAV is better if you plan to burn another audio CD at the highest quality with the songs you ripped.) Choose the High Quality option from the Setting pop-up menu.

You can always convert a song that you've already ripped in AIFF, Apple Lossless, or WAV to AAC or MP3. However, ripping a CD with one encoder might be more convenient. After that, you can rip it again with a different encoder. For example, you might import *Sgt. Pepper's Lonely Hearts Club Band* with the AAC encoder for use in your Mac and iPod and then import it again with the AIFF encoder. You might call the album Sgt. Pepper-2, for example, in order to burn songs onto an audio CD. After burning the CD, you can delete Sgt. Pepper-2 to reclaim the hard drive space.

- **AIFF Encoder:** Use AIFF if you plan to burn the song to an audio CD using a Mac (use WAV for Windows). AIFF offers the highest possible quality, but it takes up a lot of space (about 10MB per minute). Choose the Automatic option from the Setting pop-up menu for best results. Don't use AIFF format for songs that you intend to transfer to your iPod; convert them first to AAC or MP3.
- **Apple Lossless Encoder:** Use the Apple Lossless encoder for songs that you intend to burn onto audio CDs as well as for playing on iPods. The files are just small enough (about 60–70 percent of the size of the AIFF versions) that they don't hiccup on playback.

- **MP3 Encoder:** Use the MP3 format for songs that you intend to burn on MP3 CDs or that you intend to use with MP3 players or your iPod — it's universally supported. If you use MP3, I recommend choosing the Higher Quality option from the Setting pop-up menu.
- **WAV Encoder:** WAV is the high-quality sound format that's used on PCs (like AIFF), but it also takes up a lot of space (about 10MB per minute). Use WAV if you plan on burning the song to an audio CD or using WAV with PCs. Choose the Automatic option from the Setting pop-up menu for best results. Don't use WAV for songs that you intend to transfer to your iPod; use MP3 instead.

Ripping music from CDs

After checking your importing preferences to be sure that your settings are correct, you're ready to rip. To rip a CD, follow these steps:

1. **Insert an audio CD into your computer.**

   The songs appear in the List pane as generic, unnamed tracks at first. If your computer is connected to the Internet, if you've turned on the option to automatically retrieve song information from the Internet, and if the CD is in the Gracenote database (most commercial CDs are), iTunes automatically retrieves the track information.

2. **(Optional) Deselect the check boxes next to any songs on the CD that you don't want to import.**

   iTunes imports only the songs that have a check mark next to them; when you remove the check mark, iTunes skips that song.

Be sure to set your importing preferences and the Gapless Album option to your liking before actually ripping the CD.

3. **Click the Import CD button.**

   The Import CD button is at the bottom-right corner of the iTunes window. The status display shows the progress of the operation. To cancel, click the small *x* next to the progress bar in the status display.

   iTunes plays the songs while it imports them — if you previously set that option in the importing preferences. You can click the Pause button to stop playback, but the importing continues. If you don't want to listen to the songs while they import, deselect the Play Songs While Importing check box in the iTunes Preferences dialog. (See the earlier section, "Setting the importing preferences.")

If the first attempt at retrieving song information doesn't work and you see unnamed tracks, check your connection to the Internet first. If everything is fine with your connection, stop the importing operation and then choose Advanced⇨Get CD Track Names to try again to get the track information. If you don't want to connect to the Internet or if your CD isn't recognized by the Gracenote database, you can type the track information yourself.

iTunes displays an orange, animated waveform icon next to the song that it's importing. When iTunes finishes importing each song, it replaces the waveform icon with a check mark, as shown in Figure 3-4. (On a color monitor, the check mark is green.) iTunes chimes when it finishes the import list.

Figure 3-4: iTunes shows a check mark to indicate it's done ripping the song.

4. **When all the songs are imported, eject the CD by clicking the Eject button at the lower-right corner of the iTunes window.**

   You can also choose Controls⇨Eject Disc to eject the disc, or click the Eject icon next to the disc name in the Source pane.

Synchronizing Your iPod Automatically

When you set up your iPod, you can choose the option to copy your entire iTunes library automatically, matching it exactly, item for item, playlist for playlist. From that point on, your iPod synchronizes with your entire library automatically, right after you connect it to your computer.

If you make changes in iTunes after synchronizing a device, those changes are automatically made in the device when you synchronize again. If you add or delete content in your iTunes library, that content is added or deleted in the iPod when you sync again.

If you store photos in an iPhoto library (on a Mac) or in a program (such as Adobe Photoshop Album in Windows), you can set up your iPod with the option to copy your entire photo library. Your iPod is then synchronized automatically so that any changes you make to the photo library are copied to the device.

Content items stored *remotely* (such as songs shared from other iTunes libraries on a network) aren't synchronized because the files aren't physically on your computer.

To prevent an iPod from automatically synchronizing, press ⌘-Option (Mac) or Ctrl-Alt (Windows) while you connect the device, and then keep pressing until the iPod name appears in the iTunes Source pane.

Follow these steps to start synchronizing your iPod with your iTunes library:

1. **With iTunes running, connect the iPod or iPhone, and then select its name when it appears in the Devices section of the Source pane.**

   iTunes displays the device's Summary page (under the Summary tab of the device's synchronization pages) to the right of the Source pane, which includes how much space on the device is occupied by content and how much is still free, as shown in Figure 3-5.

2. **If the iPod isn't automatically synchronizing, click the Sync button in the bottom-right corner to synchronize it.**

   The iTunes Status pane tells you that iTunes is syncing the device.

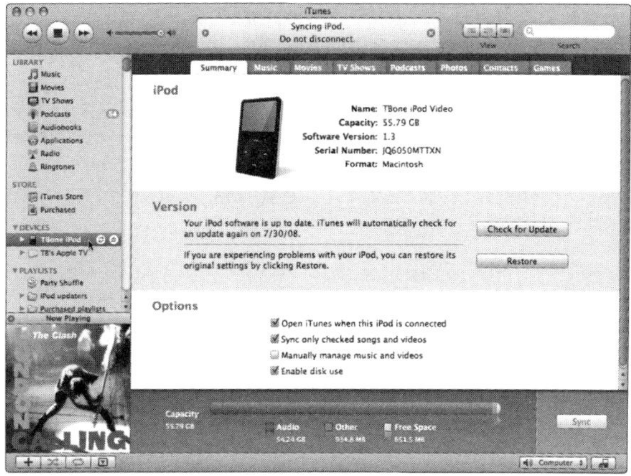

Figure 3-5: The iPod Summary tab.

3. **Wait for the synchronization to finish and then click the Eject button next to the iPod name in the Source pane.**

   You should always wait until the iTunes Status pane (at the top) displays that the synchronization is finished.

4. **Disconnect your iPod from your computer.**

   Don't disconnect your iPod until its menu appears in its display.

   That's it. Your iPod is now synchronized.

If your iTunes library is too large to fit on your iPod, you can still keep your iPod automatically synchronized to a subset of your library. For example, you can update the iPod automatically but only with selected songs, movies, TV shows, videos, audio books, or podcast episodes. To use this method, you must first *deselect* the items in your iTunes library that you don't want to transfer, because all the items in your library are selected by default.

To deselect an item, click the check box next to the item in the List pane so that the check mark disappears. To select an item, click the check box so that the check mark appears.

Alternatively, you can change your iPod's Music settings to update by certain playlists. That way, any changes you make to those playlists — adding or deleting songs, for example — are reflected in your iPod the next time you synchronize it to your computer. After selecting the iPod in the Source pane, click the Music tab and select the Sync Music and Selected Playlists options. From the Selected Playlists list box, select each playlist you want to include in the synchronization with your iPod. Click Apply to apply the changes and sync your iPod. iTunes automatically synchronizes the device by erasing its contents and copying only the playlists that you selected.

Synchronizing by playlist is useful, especially if you define a set of playlists in your iTunes library to use just for synchronizing with a particular iPod. I synchronize different iPods to different sets of playlists so that I can maintain one iTunes library for several iPods.

Appendix
Solving Basic iPod Problems

In This Appendix

- Getting your iPod to respond
- Keeping your battery juiced
- Last ditch troubleshooting

Even though I think the iPod comes as close to perfection as possible, at some point your iPod isn't going to work as you expect it to. This appendix shows you how to fix the most common problems.

Waking Up Your iPod

If your iPod doesn't turn on, don't panic. Try these methods to get your iPod to respond:

- **Check the Hold switch's position on top of the iPod.** Slide the Hold switch so that it hides the orange layer to unlock the buttons.
- **See whether the iPod has enough juice.** Is the battery charged? Connect the iPod to a power source and see whether it works.
- **Reset your iPod if it still doesn't turn on.** See "Reset the iPod" a little later in this appendix.

Making the Battery Last

Here are some things you can do to keep your battery going longer:

- **Press the Play/Pause button to pause (stop) playback.** If you simply turn off your car or home stereo and remove your headphones without pausing playback, your iPod continues playing until the playlist or album ends. When playback is paused, the power-save feature turns off the iPod after two minutes of inactivity.
- **Press and hold the Play/Pause button to turn off the iPod when you're not using it.** Rather than waiting for two minutes of inactivity for the power-save feature to turn off the iPod, turn it off yourself and save battery time.
- **Turn off the backlighting.** If you don't need to use backlighting, turn it off.
- **Set the Hold switch to lock when you're not using the iPod.** Keep your iPod controls locked so the iPod doesn't turn on accidentally.

Reset the iPod

Sometimes when your iPod refuses to turn on, you can fix it by resetting. This operation resets the operating system of the iPod and restarts the system.

For fourth-, fifth-, and sixth-generation iPods, iPod nano, fourth-generation iPods, iPod mini, and iPod U2 Special Edition, follow these steps:

1. **(Optional) Connect the iPod to a power outlet by using the AC power adapter.**
2. **Push the Hold switch to lock, and then push it back to unlock.**
3. **Press and hold the Menu and Select buttons simultaneously for at least six seconds or until the Apple logo appears; then release the buttons.**

For first-, second-, and third-generation iPod models, follow these steps:

1. **(Optional) Connect the iPod to a power outlet by using the AC power adapter.**
2. **Push the Hold switch to lock, and then push it back to unlock.**
3. **Press and hold the Menu and Play/Pause buttons simultaneously for at least five seconds until the Apple logo appears; then release the buttons.**

To reset your iPod shuffle, disconnect it from a computer, and switch the slider on the back to the Off position — the green stripe under the switch should not be visible. Wait five seconds and then switch the slider back to On.

After resetting, everything should be back to normal, including your music and data files.

Restoring to Factory Conditions

If all else fails, you can try *restoring* your iPod. Restoring an iPod erases the hard drive and returns the device to its factory settings.

To restore an iPod, follow these steps for both the Mac and Windows versions of iTunes:

1. **Connect the iPod to your computer.**

   iTunes opens automatically.

2. **Select the iPod in the Devices section of the Source pane, and click the Summary tab (Settings tab for an iPod shuffle) if it is not already selected.**

   The device's Summary/Settings page appears.

3. **Click the Restore button.**

   An alert dialog appears to confirm that you want to restore the device.

4. **Click the Restore button again to confirm the restore operation.**

   A progress bar appears, indicating the progress of the restore operation.

5. **For some iPod models, follow the instructions to disconnect your iPod and connect it to an AC power adapter, if required.**

   iTunes notifies you when the restore is finished.

6. **Synchronize your iPod with content from your iTunes library.**

   You need to put back all the content you erased!

7. **When you finish synchronizing the iPod with content and data, eject the device by clicking the Eject button.**

With more than 1,400 titles to choose from, we've got a Dummies book for wherever you are in life!

Business/Personal Finance & Investment

Title	ISBN	Price
High-Powered Investing All-in-One For Dummies	9780470186268	$29.99
Investing For Dummies, 5th Edition	9780470289655	$21.99
Living Well in a Down Economy For Dummies	9780470401170	$14.99
Managing Your Money All-in-One For Dummies	9780470345467	$29.99
Personal Finance Workbook For Dummies	9780470099339	$19.99
Taxes 2009 For Dummies (January 2009)	9780470249512	$17.99

Crafts & Hobbies

Title	ISBN	Price
California Wine For Dummies (May 2009)	9780470376072	$16.99
Canning & Preserving For Dummies	9780764524714	$16.99
Jewelry & Beading Designs For Dummies	9780470291122	$19.99
Knitting For Dummies, 2nd Edition	9780470287477	$21.99
Quilting For Dummies, 2nd Edition	9780764597992	$21.99
Watercolor Painting For Dummies	9780470182314	$24.99

Fitness & Diet

Title	ISBN	Price
Dieting For Dummies, 2nd Edition	9780764541490	$21.99
Low-Calorie Dieting For Dummies	9780764599057	$21.99
Nutrition For Dummies, 4th Edition	9780471798682	$21.99
Exercise Balls For Dummies	9780764556234	$21.99
Fitness For Dummies, 3rd Edition	9780764578519	$21.99
Stretching For Dummies	9780470067413	$16.99